With My Very Best Wishes

John Newell.

Bahrain.

Now & *Then*
BAHRAIN

H.H. Shaikh Salman Bin Hamad Al Khalifa
The Crown Prince

H.H. Shaikh Khalifa Bin Salman Al Khalifa
The Prime Minister

H.H. Shaikh Hamad Bin Isa Al Khalifa
The Amir of the State of Bahrain

His Highness Shaikh Isa Bin Salman Al-Khalifa
The Late Amir

"The late Amir Sheikh Isa Bin Salman Al Khalifa with his sons at Bahrain Interarntional Airport".

Our Earth Series
Volume IV
By John J. Nowell LRPS FRGS

Foreword

With the approach of the new millennium, it is perhaps appropriate that we, the people of Bahrain, both Nationals and expatriates, should look back at our achievements over the last millennium.

A Bahraini citizen, born in 1904, is portrayed within these pages. He, more than any of us, has witnessed the entire spectrum of changes. From his childhood spent during the years of the First World War, his years spent as a Nakoudah at the pearl beds, the arrival of the first aeroplanes and on to the present day. He tells of occasions when very important people would indicate to him that they wished to be taken to Manama by dhow. He saw the arrival of the swing bridge and the first causeway, the demise of the pearl industry and the discovery of oil. With the Second World War, he saw the influx of allied troops and the flood of oil workers. With oil revenues came schools, hospitals, modern housing, new mosques and jet air travel. To his great credit, he maintained his dhows and maritime lifestyle and passed his skills on to his son who now uses his traditional dhows to convey tourists and expatriates alike to our beautiful islands.

It is at this point, where my responsibilities as the Minister of Housing, Municipalities and the Environment lay. The need to maintain a balance between housing and our beautiful environment is a delicate one and one that we should all strive to preserve.

This beautiful book covers the entire spectrum of the events that have changed our islands forever. Events that have led to the standards of living, health, education and prosperity that we enjoy today. Readers should absorb the hidden message within these stunning pages. I would ask readers to reflect on their individual responsibilities to enjoy their lives to the full but to protect the environment for the new millennium.

Sheikh Khalid bin Abdallah AL Khalifa,
Minister of Housing, Municipalities and
Environment.

Our Earth Series

Now & *Then*
BAHRAIN

Our Earth Series
Volume IV
John J. Nowell LRPS FRGS

ميراكـل جـرافيكس
miracle graphics

ZODIAC PUBLISHING LLC

A joint venture publication by Zodiac Publishing in
association with Miracle Graphics Printing & Publishing.

Zodiac Publishing,
P.O.Box 35121, Dubai.
Tel: 09714 - 2826966 Fax: 09714 - 2826882.
E-mail: jjnowell@emirates.net.ae.
Web site: www.soorah.com.

Miracle Graphics Printing & Publishing,
P.O.Box 743, Manama, Bahrain.
Tel: 0973 - 715500, Fax: 0973 - 716685
E-mail: miracle@batelco.com.bh

First published 1999.
First reprint 2001.

Copyright John J. Nowell 1999.

Other books in the series:

A Day Above Oman.
A Day Above The Emirates.
A Day Above Yemen.

Now & Then -The Emirates.
Now & Then Dubai.
Now & Then Abu Dhabi.

ISBN 0-9533034-0-3

British Library Cataloguing-in-Publication Data.
A catalogue record for this book is available
from the British Library.

Design by Nick Crawley of Zodiac Publishing.
Printing by Emirates Printing Press.
"Now & Then" is a Zodiac Publishing registered trademark.

Contents

BAHRAIN IS AN ARCHIPELAGO OF 36 ISLANDS, with a total land area of 706 sq. kms. Its name is derived from two Arabic words 'thnain bahr' meaning 'two seas'. This name refers to the phenomenon of sweet water springs under the sea, which mingle with the salty seawater. This combination is believed to be responsible for the unusual lustre of Bahrain's natural pearls. Many natural freshwater springs once irrigated the fertile north and western areas of Bahrain from underground aquifers. Just as the oil under the sands is finite, the water will not flow forever; estimates in most places are that it will last less than 50 years.

Pages 8-9. TRADE HAS BEEN THE INTERNATIONAL factor in the development of Bahrain. Traditional dhows could carry 200 tons of cargo but now these are dwarfed by the huge container ships, which now dock at Mina Salman. Such container vessels weigh more than 50,000 tons and are capable of carrying more than 4000 containers.

Pages 10-11. THE BAHRAIN NATIONAL MUSEUM lies beyond the busy crossroads leading to the causeway to Muharraq. Within the museum, ancient artefacts from Bahrain's historical sites, life size exhibits including a burial mound, with 5000-year-old skeletons and pottery and scenes from the recent past are displayed. There are more than 150,000 burial mounds on Bahrain covering a variety of periods. Strategically located between Mesopotamia and the Indus Valley, Dilmun developed a strong political, economic and a social structure in this period. Today, interest is developing in many other aspects of the history of Bahrain. One of the next projects is to convert the old British Embassy, shown here on the old waterfront, into a museum.

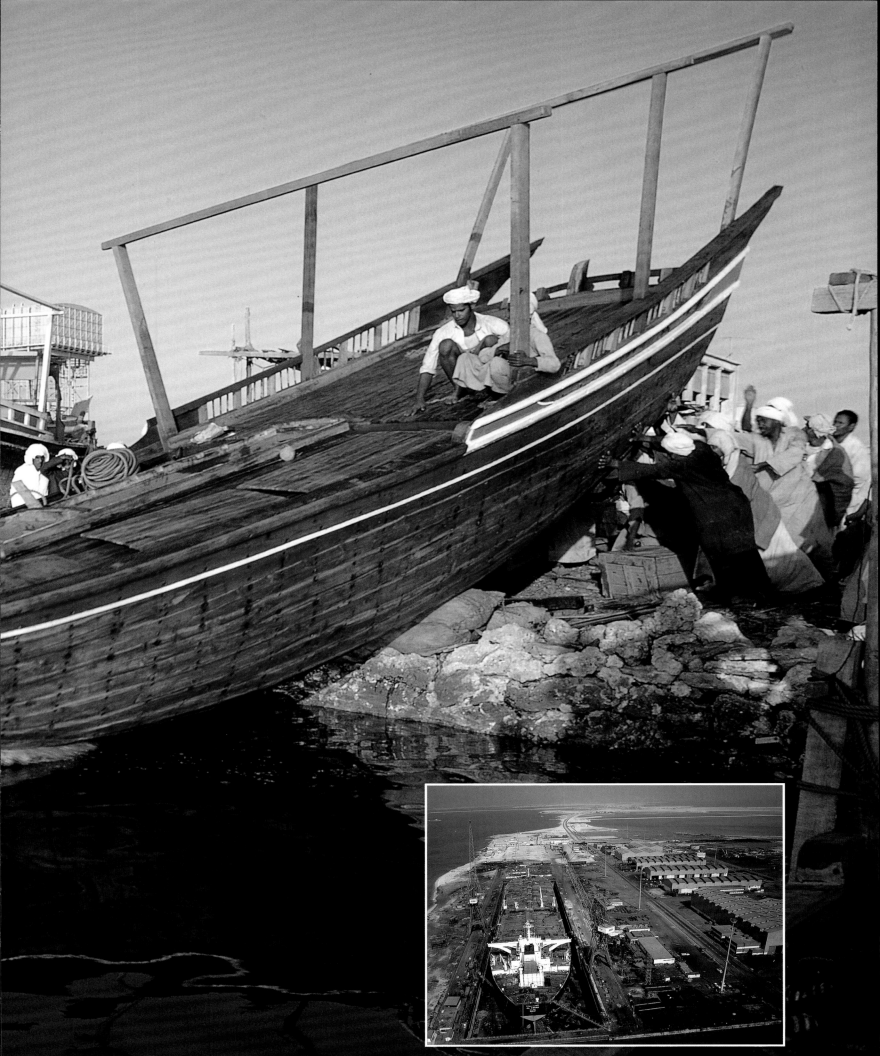

NO ONE REALLY KNOWS WERE THEY CAME FROM. THE FIRST HUMANS probably crossed the land bridge between the mainland and Bahrain at the end of the last Ice Age, some 10,000 years ago. Man was not the first occupant of this land. 65 million years ago, dinosaurs roamed through what was a lush tropical land. Recently, geologists from Sultan Qaboos University in Muscat have discovered remains of dinosaurs dating back to the prehistoric era, which is said to be the first discovery of its kind in this region. Such a find indicates the existence of extensive forests over what is now the Arabian Peninsula though the shape of the peninsula would be vastly different to the present shape. The remains found by the geologists appear to be that of the carnivorous Therapods and the herbivore Sauropods. The Sauropods were giant, four legged, long-necked creatures, which roamed the earth in the late Cretaceous period, some 66 -100 million years ago. The remains of the forests were laid down, over millions of years, in formations that eventually formed the oil reserves that we rely on today.

We know that for at least 7000 years and probably much longer, people have lived on Bahrain. For most of that time, they left no written records, no accounts of what they did or how they lived. However, things they made, things they threw away, even their bones remain to tell us of their lives and doings. During the Stone Age period, lasting approximately 2000 years (5000 BC to 3200 BC), fishermen and hunters roamed Bahrain. Their tools and weapons of flint have survived to this day while those of wood and bone have largely disappeared. In other parts of the world, the first cities were being built; in Mesopotamia, the Indus Valley and China. Trading with overseas countries and societies slowly developed and the need to travel encouraged advances in ship and dhow building. Ships called at Bahrain to replenish their fresh water supplies and left shards of pottery among the Stone Age flints.

In the Formative Dilmun period, (3200 BC to 2200 BC), there was initially only a huddle of stone houses along the shore with a watering place for merchant ships who traded copper for pearls. Then gradually, Dilmun grew, building its own boats and its own trade network. As always, wealth brought growing danger and at some time, late in this period, the defenceless town was attacked and burnt to the ground.

The Barbar Temple, a 3rd millennium structure, was excavated in the 1950's and shows the high degree of civilisation of the Bahraini people at that time. The discovery revealed important aspects of their religious practices and mythology. The findings included a bronze bull's head - strongly resembling Sumerian artistry and similar to that found in the Royal grave of Ur. The bull's head, an ancient Middle Eastern symbol of divinity, may have been a decoration for a lyre (musical instrument). Other findings include an alabaster jar - possibly Egyptian and numerous Dilmun seals made of soapstone depicting my thological subjects. These

are now on display at the Bahrain national museum. The temple consists of large stones, specifically cut for their purpose, which came from nearby Jidda Island. Three distinct layers were each built at different stages of the temple's existence, in a style similar to that found in Mesopotamia (Iraq). The temple proper consists of a main courtyard where the stones are aligned in a circle believed to represent the sacrificial altar. Stones nearby were probably used for tethering the sacrificial animals. A staircase leads down to a sweet water well. The temple is believed to be related to the worship of Enki – God of sweet water and wisdom, the main deity of Dilmun (ancient Bahrain). Enki was worshiped by the Sumerians in Mesopotamia and Sumerian records indicate that Dilmun was Enki's home and Holy Land. In the Early Dilmun Period, (2200 BC to 1600 BC) protective walls were built around the town. These were centuries of prosperity based on rich sea trade. Strategically located between Mesopotamia and the Indus Valley, Dilmun developed a strong political, economic and social structure during this period. From India to the Mediterranean, the Dilmun stamp seals were known and respected. Temples were built and burial mounds in their thousands constructed, the royal mounds at A'Ali towering above the rest. There are more than 150,000 burial mounds on Bahrain dating from a variety of periods. The mounds cover 30 sq.km or 5% of the main island of Bahrain. Generally, adults were placed in the main chamber while children were placed in a subsidiary chamber, outside the ringwall. A complete mound was transported to the Bahrain Natural History Museum where it is now displayed. The Saar Burial Complex (2200BC – 1600BC) consists of about 1500 subterranean burial chambers, separated from each other by interconnected curved stone walks. Each chamber contains the remains of an adult man or woman, lying in a flexed position, normally on the right side. The complex was constructed about the same time as the Late Dilmun mound fields but may have been used by people of lower economic or social status since the cost of these simple constructions would be far less than a burial mound. In this type of burial complex children could not be buried outside the ringwalls and hence a special section for children was created.

By the Middle Dilmun Period, from 1600 BC to 1000 BC, Bahrain became increasingly dependent upon Mesopotamia. In about 1400 BC, the Kassite Kings of Babylon took control of Bahrain, increasing the structure of the city walls and building massive stone storehouses. After 250 years, the Kassite dynasty in Mesopotamia was overthrown and their rule in Bahrain ended. In the Late Dilmun Period, from 1000 BC to 330 BC, independent Kings ruled Bahrain. except for a 60-year period of Assyrian domination. Wealth from the continuing pearl trade and the new incense trade financed the building of the palace at Ras AI-Qalah whose walls still stand.

Greek culture entered the Gulf during the Tylos Period, (330 BC to 630AD) and although the Greek name of Tylos was adopted, Bahrain was never actually part of the Greek Empire. During this period the continuing demand for the incense trade brought Bahrain into closer contact with mainland Arabia and other civilizations and religions of the outside world.

In 622 AD Bahrain embraced Islam. Missionaries from the mainland of Arabia converted the people of Bahrain during the lifetime of the Prophet (PBUH). This was a time of prosperity when Bahrain maintained close contact with other Islamic centres. The first Masjid Al Khamis Mosque was built during this period; it is the oldest mosque in Bahrain and reflects that Bahrain turned to Islam at a very early stage. It was later extended and the now famous and distinctive twin minarets were added in the fifteenth century. The famous Thursday market, known from monochrome photographs, was held there until the 1960's. Today the mosque is being renovated and on completion the surrounding area will once again be used as a market, principally for tourists.

During the Middle Islamic period, seafaring trade increased considerably. Bahrain together with other ports around the Gulf was involved in the India and China trade. This increase in trade involved long and difficult ocean voyages. The Arabs of the Gulf developed their own system of navigation based on astronomy. They absorbed and in many cases surpassed the work of the Chinese and Greek scholars in this field setting down their knowledge in navigational documents. For instance, the Bahraini seafarers knew all about the astrolabe and magnetic compass. They also used an instrument known as the kashaba. This revolutionary device, the forerunner of the sextant, was a hand-held wooden sighting instrument used to determine position by taking a fix on the Pole Star relative to the horizon.

As in previous centuries, success in trade brought foreign intervention and Iran, Oman and Portugal held Bahrain from time to time. Arad Fort was probably built at the end of the 16th century. Its location was determined by its ability to guard the deep-water channel adjacent to Muharraq and Manama. At this time, Arad had a better strategic position than the Bahrain ('Portuguese') fort, since the small Abu Mahir fort on the other side of Muharraq Bay reinforced its defences. The fort was first built with a double wall then developed by the Omanis in 1800. The Al Khalifa recaptured it after a few years of occupation by the Omanis. Riffa Fort was built by Sheikh Sulman bin Ahmed Al Fateh in 1812 and was used as a military fort before becoming a private residence until the 1970s. It was renovated in 1989.

In recent years, the Bahrain government has taken steps to preserve and display its heritage. The National Museum lies beyond the busy crossroads leading to the causeway to Muharraq. Ancient artifacts from

Bahrain's historical sites are displayed within the museum together with life size exhibits including a burial mound complete with 5000-year-old skeletons, pottery and scenes from the recent past.

Bahrain has distinguished itself since the days of old by its highly skilled handicrafts. The scripts of Dilmun and the artifacts found during the excavation of the burial mounds show the skilled workmanship of the earlier craftsmen. The attention given to Bahrain's traditional crafts stems from the desire of the leaders of this country to preserve this aspect of Bahrain's heritage as an essential ingredient of the nation's cultural landmarks. It is a source of national pride extending from the past into the present. Bahrain's traditional artisans have inherited, innovated, and manually processed various works of art using a variety of materials, from pottery to gold. Through participation in regional and international exhibitions, they have received recognition and merits world-wide. Traditional crafts in Bahrain received further enhancement with the Government's establishment of the AI-Jasra Handicraft Centre in 1990. Bait Al Jasra, H.H. the late Amir's birthplace, was built in 1907 and restored as a heritage museum in 1986. This centre has enabled artisans to produce, market and promote their products. Their previous individual status is now characterised by teamwork in an environment where they can innovate and produce within a sound commercial atmosphere. The main objective of the AI-Jasra Handicraft Centre is to preserve the national identity of Bahrain's heritage and to improve the quality of products so that these crafts may stand as a strong symbol of the country's ancient past. Therefore, every effort is made to develop the craftsmanship of artisans and to provide every available resource. Arrangements are also made to offer these traditionally manufactured products for sale at various outlets in Bahrain.

Thus, the cycle turns full circle. Foreign visitors now fly into Bahrain to enjoy the warmth and hospitality of this delightful country. They come armed with cameras to capture the sights and sounds of this ancient land. They come to dive into the multicoloured seas, wearing state of the art scuba gear instead of the dugong nose clips and simple cotton coveralls of yesteryear. Each sport diver can take his own harvest of oysters from the sea bed, open these on the deck of the diving boat and keep any pearls he finds. It seems ironic that the 10,000-year cycle has reached the present day by way of the discovery of oil, jets from Gulf Air, motorbikes, cultured pearls and tankers sailing around the world. At the time of publication, only a few hundred sport diving tourists have taken advantage of the exciting opportunity to find their own pearls. However, to the credit of the organisers, every diver has returned home having found a natural pearl, even if only a small one. The beauty of a natural pearl is something that a cultured pearl can only attempt to replace; it is something that has grown for hundreds and thousands of years and continues to grow to this day in the unique environment that is Bahrain's two seas.

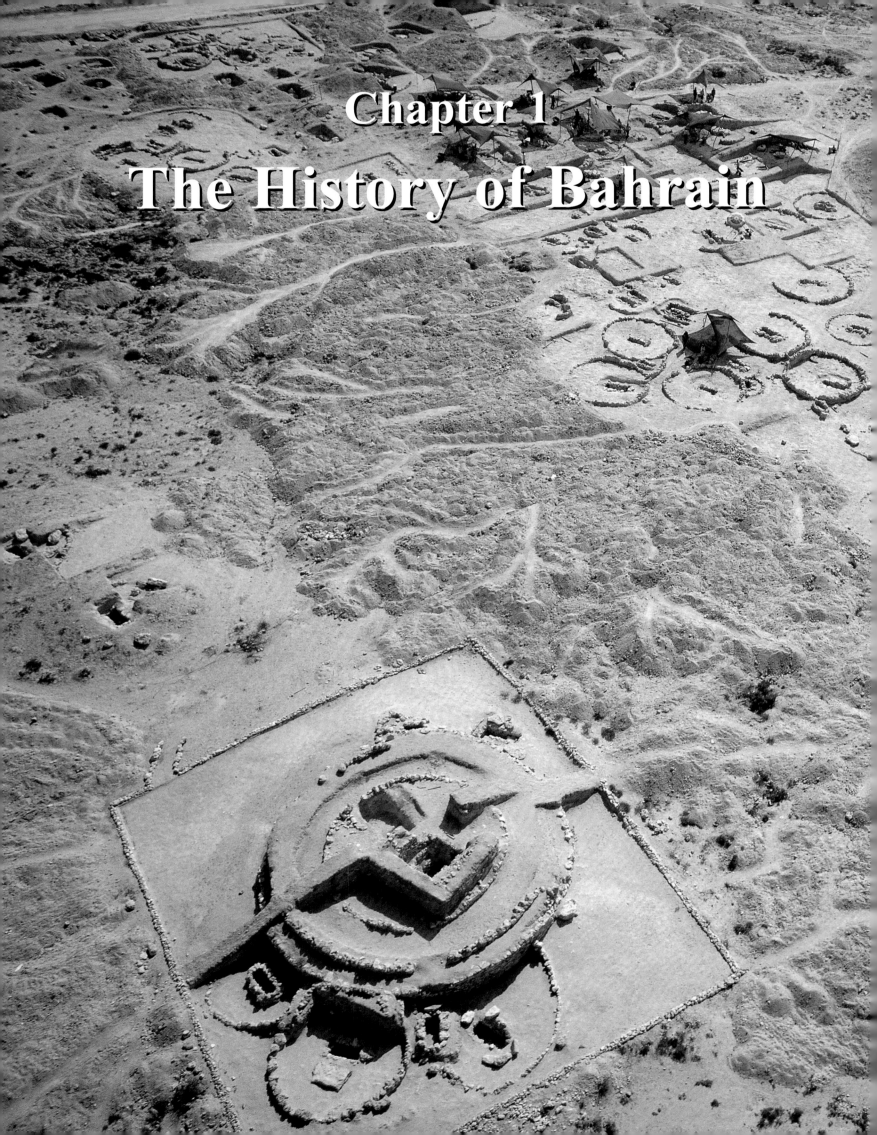

Chapter 1
The History of Bahrain

BAHRAIN ONCE HAD THE LARGEST PREHISTORIC CEMETERY
in the world, when an estimated 150,000 burial mounds
covered the central and western areas. Archaeological
finds of those uncovered, reveal evidence of two distinct
civilizations, the Dilmun and Tylos — two thousand
years apart, dating from the third and first millennia.

THE BARBAR TEMPLE, A 3RD MILLENNIUM STRUCTURE, was excavated in the 1950's and shows the high degree of civilisation of the Bahrain people at that time. The discovery revealed important aspects of their religious practices and mythology. The findings included a bronze bull's head — similar to that found in the Royal grave of Ur. The bull's head, an ancient Middle Eastern symbol of divinity, may have been a decoration for a lyre (musical instrument). Other findings include alabaster jars — possibly Egyptian and numerous Dilmun seals made of soapstone depicting mythological subjects. These are now on display at the Bahrain national museum.

The temple consists of large stones, specifically cut for their purpose, which came from nearby Jidda Island. Three distinct layers were each built at different stages in a style similar to that of Mesopotamia (Iraq). The temple proper consists of a main courtyard where the stones are aligned in a circle believed to represent the sacrificial altar. Stones nearby were probably for tethering the sacrificial animals.

A staircase leads down to a sweet water well. The temple is believed to be related to the worship of Enki — God of sweet water and wisdom, the main deity of Dilmun (ancient Bahrain). Enki was worshipped by the Sumerians in Mesopotamia and Sumerian records indicate that Dilmun was Enki's Holy Land and home.

FROM A VEHICLE, TRAVELLERS DRIVING FROM MANAMA
towards to the King Fahad Causeway may be oblivious
to the fact that they are passing Saar, one of the
world's most amazing archaeological discoveries. From
a helicopter, the view of the excavated city unfolds.
Here are houses, streets and a well surrounding a
central temple. The site was excavated by the London-
Bahrain Archaeological Expedition in 1989 and their
detailed report records that the settlement was
inhabited by a population numbering between 300-400
between 2100 and 1800BC. This period was during
the Dilmun era when Bahrain was a vital transit point
in the copper trade between Oman and southern Iraq.
The temple roof was carried on three columns which
are clearly visble on the aerial photograph. The temple
is surrounded by a wide main street which in turn,
leads to a series of narrow streets of two- or three-
roomed houses.

THE MOSQUE AL-KHAMIS IS THE OLDEST MOSQUE in Bahrain. The people of Bahrain converted to Islam during the life of the Prophet Mohammed (PBUH). The Mosque Al Khamis is the oldest mosque in Bahrain; it has been rebuilt on a number of occasions. The distinctive twin minarets were added during the fifteenth century. The famous Thursday market, show on the monochrome photographs, was held until the 1960's. Today the mosque is being renovated and the surrounding area will be once again used as a market, principally for tourists.

THE TYLOS FORT AT RAS AL QALAH, ON THE northern shore of Bahrain, was slowly eroded by the sea and replaced in the 14th century by a new one built further inland. At that time, Bahrain was part of the commercial empire in the Gulf dominated by the Princes of Hormuz. In 1506, Portugal appointed a new viceroy and governor, Alfonso da Albuquerque, to consolidate their growing Indian Ocean possessions. When the Portuguese invaded Hormuz in 1507, they quickly realised the strategic position of Bahrain. The pearl trade and the vital water supply were irresistible to the Portuguese and, having captured Bahrain, commenced a restructuring programme of the fort. The fort was originally built during the 14th century on European medieval lines, roughly square with high walls buttressed by towers. In 1561, the Portuguese architect, Inofne de Carvalho, reinforced the fort by building three bastions. The fort was adapted to new developments in military technology and 'boulevards,' contained by an outer wall, encircled the fort. The Portuguese rule was brief however and in 1602, the Persians captured the fort.

WITH THE EXPULSION OF THE PORTUGUESE,
Bahrain entered a relatively stable period and it
was not until the discovery of oil that any major
changes were visible. The oil income was spent
discreetly and wisely. Fine new mosques were
built and in 1943 the government opened the
first state-supported religious school. The men
displaced by the decline in pearling were helped
to find other employment, and fishing increased
in importance. Most immediately evident was
the physical transformation which was taking
place, and which these photographs very clearly
demonstrate. Roads were paved, less romantic
looking concrete or limestone replaced barasti
houses, and public buildings began to transform
the Manama waterfront. The Customs House
was opened in the 1920's, the new Court House
in the 1930's, and the swing bridge after the end
of the Second World War.

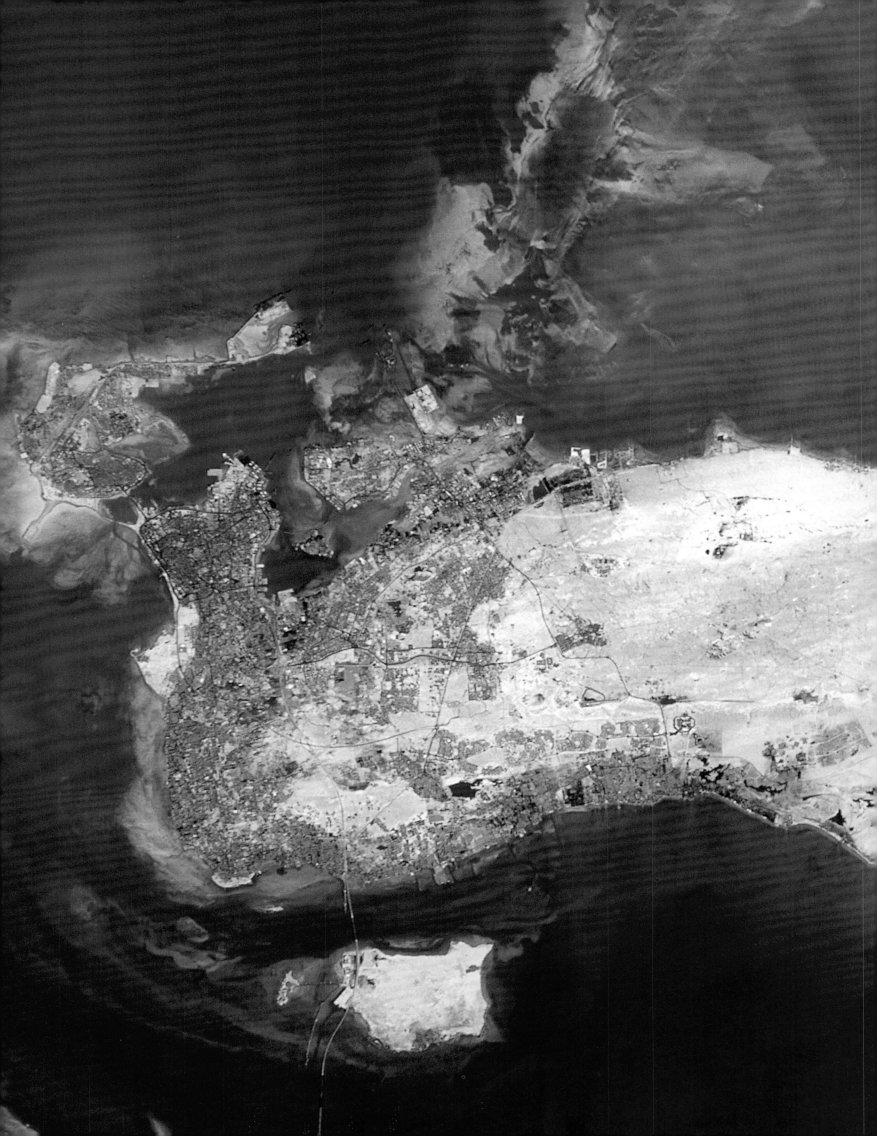

MOST SPACE SHUTTLE FLIGHTS PASS OVER THE Middle East with a transit time from Egypt to Muscat of just four minutes. Even when flying free of the space shuttle, the astronaut is travelling at an amazing 25,000mph, 165 miles above the Earth. The astronauts fly over the "Fertile Crescent", the area between the Tigris River in Iraq and the Nile in Egypt, where agriculture began in the ninth millennium BC and where urban societies arose in the fifth millennium BC. Their next view from space is of Bahrain where the delicate greenery of the extensive date plantations is clearly visible. In days of yore, the nakudahs (captains) of sailing dhows would see the same plantation from a different angle.

Chapter 2
Of Sails & Pearls

THE WARM SHALLOW WATERS SURROUNDING THE
Bahrain archipelago nurture the most prolific
oyster beds in the Gulf. Diving for pearls has
taken place throughout the whole of recorded
history. In the Sumerian Epic of Gilgamesh, a
pearl of Dilmun represented the secret of
eternal life. It was given to Gilgamesh, a hero
who was part man, part beast, but he dropped it
in the sea where it was swallowed by a serpent.
It was during the Roman period that pearls
reached their ascendant position. Pliny, in his
writings noted that"Our ladies glory in having
pearls suspended from their fingers, one or two
or three of them dangling from their ears,
delighted even with the rattling of the pearls as
they knock against each other. I once saw Lollia
Paulina (died in AD 48), the wife of the
Emperor Gaius, covered with emeralds and
pearls, which shone in alternate layers upon her
head, in her hair, in her wreaths, in her ears,
upon her neck, in her bracelets, and on her
fingers".

To put this description into realistic perspective,
one excellent, and two or three good pearl
necklaces would be the result of three-month
diving season for one boat crew consisting of 10
- 20 men diving constantly during daylight
hours. The photograph above was taken in
1912, when the French jeweller Jacques Cartier
came to visit Sheikh Isa on Muharraq to buy
pearls. The visiting pearl merchants usually
stayed in what became know as the Bait Skinner
House, now demolished.

WHEN PEARLING WAS AT ITS HEIGHT IN THE 1800S, THE MOST IMPORTANT manufacturing industry in Bahrain was the building of dhows. It was the very essence of trade that dhows returned from far flung places with a cargo of timbers and other items needed to build more boats. Only the shashah was made entirely from parts of the local date palm. Teak (saj) for the keel, stem, stern planking and masts of the larger boats was brought from India. mit from Iran and Iraq or Somalia was used to form the ribs and knees. Finally, rope from Zanzibar was bound to the sail canvas, made locally in Bahrain, to complete the finished dhow.

THE DIVERS WORE A LOINCLOTH OR SOMETIMES an overall cotton garment as a protection against the stings of jellyfish, their only equipment was a nose-clip made from dugong bone. Each diver's mate worked two ropes: one was weighted and the other carried a basket. The diver put his foot in a loop of the weighted rope and held the basket rope. He then sank with the weight to the bottom. The diver released the weighted rope, which was pulled up to the surface. Whilst he held his breath the diver gathered as many shells as he could, then tugged the second rope as a signal to his mate to haul him up. By this means, they fished at depths of up to sixty feet, diving again and again and collecting perhaps a dozen shells each time.

The main photograph shows a page from the pearling log, which recorded each diver's account with the 'Nakhuda.' This was one of the principal reforms introduced by Sheikh Hamad bin Isa, together with strict limits on the amount of interest which captains could charge their crews for advances against their eventual share in the profits of the season.

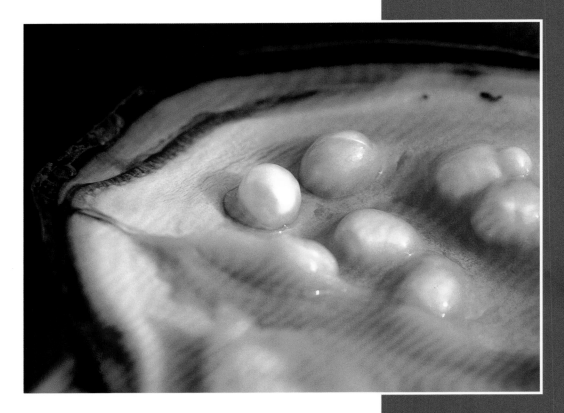

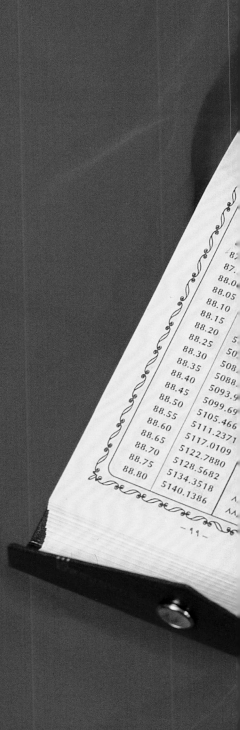

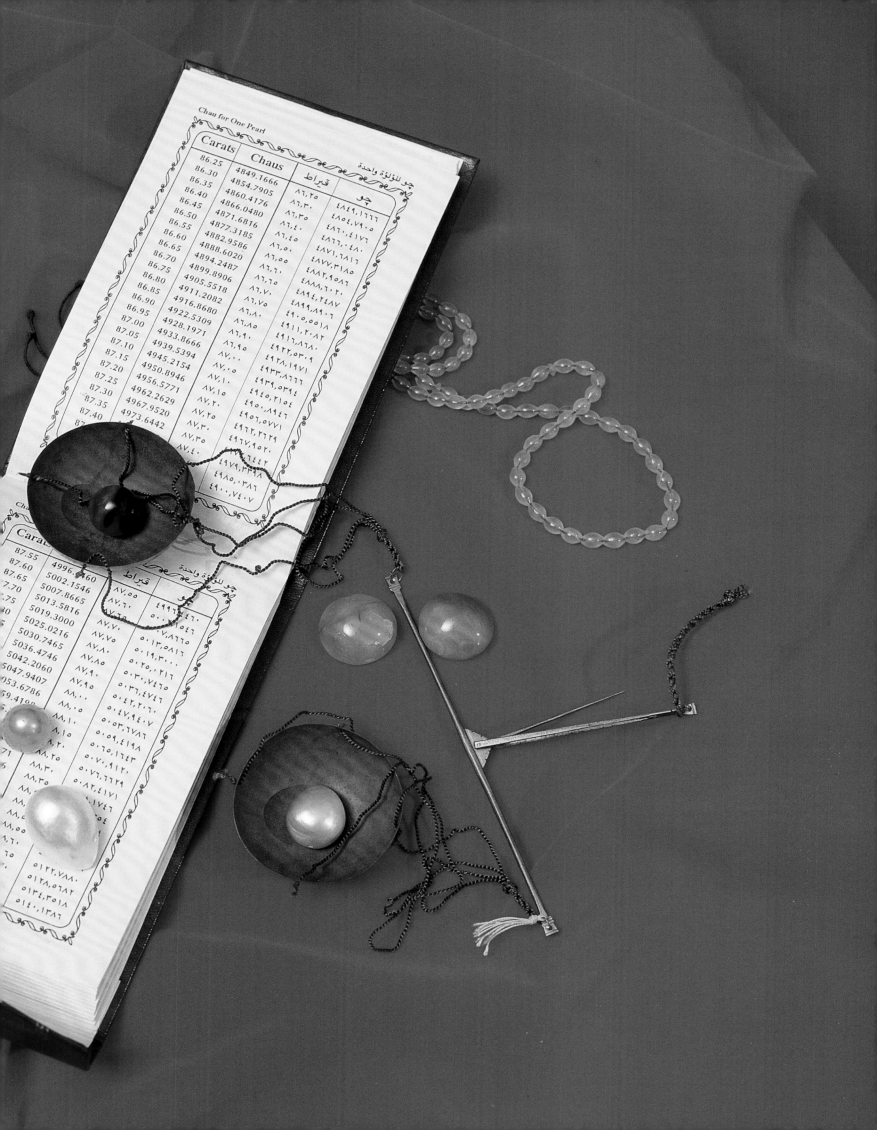

PEARLING OCCUPIED THOUSANDS OF THE
SMALLER dhows — sambuks, shu'ais and
jaliboots — for four or five months in the
summer of every year. In the 19th century,
1500 boats would go out from Bahrain alone,
and uncounted others from Kuwait, Qatar and
the coastal villages of Saudi Arabia. Divers
were a community apart from other men, with
songs and rites and dances of their own. On the
appointed departure day, the sailors and divers
would embark to the beat of drums and all set
sail together. Today, the same traditions exist
and can be seen almost every afternoon when
the dhow fishing fleet departs to the north
against a backdrop of the sun setting over the
Le Royal Meridien Hotel.

IN 1905, THERE WERE ABOUT 15000 DIVERS OUT OF THE BAHRAIN population of 99,000 and whole areas depended on the pearling trade. Most divers lived on Muharraq Island with 5582 in Muharraq Town, 3146 in Hidd and 1172 on Halat Naim and Halat Sulutah. Many more lived on Manama with 1482 concentrated in Budaiya.

No direct taxes were levied on pearls or pearl divers apart from modest boat registration licenses. Indirectly, Bahrain State

revenue depended on a healthy pearl trade. When the trade prospered, more people bought imported, taxed goods that in turn provided the main income of the State. In 1928, pearling and customs produced Rs. 1,124,000 out of a total reserve of R. 1,215,000. In 1929, pearling was prospering, with 538 boats and 20,000 divers. Terminal decline began in 1930 with the world depression and the introduction of Japanese cultured pearls. Fortunately, oil was discovered in 1932 to provide employment. By 1954, there were only 11 boats and 538 divers.

SINCE THE FIRST HUMANS REACHED BAHRAIN OVER 10,000 years ago, the warm waters of the Arabian Gulf and the Arabian Sea have played an indispensable part in the life of the people, both as a source of food and fresh water. As their civilisation developed, Bahrain's boat builders and seafarers became renowned for their skills in construction and navigation. Dhows reached as far as China and all the areas including the Gulf and the Indian Ocean. However, Bahrain's most vital products were its pearls. Today, modern tourist are as keen to dive for a pearl as the first divers were some 6000 years ago. This new attraction is likely to be regarded, in retrospect, as the most highly significant new tourist adventure.

Chapter 3
The Arrival of Aviation

AFTER THE FIRST WORLD WAR, IT WAS CONSIDERED VITAL BY THE British Government to establish air communication throughout the Empire. In 1918, Major General W. G. Salmond of the Royal Flying Corps flew from Cairo to Delhi in less than 48 hours flying time. The following year, in 1919, Ross & Keith Smith flew from England to Australia via Persia and India in less than thirty days. During the same year, 1919, Sheikh Abdullah bin Isa and Sheikh Moh'd bin Abdullah became the first Bahrainis to fly in an aircraft in England. Diplomatic problems with Persia prompted the British Government to explore the potential of a route along the southern Gulf. In 1920, the British Civil Commissioner from Baghdad arrived in to explore the possibility of creating an aerodrome in Bahrain. The archives show that "an aeroplane ground and plot measuring 650 yards long (592 metres) and 400 yards (364 metres) broad with T-cloth to indicate wind direction" was to be laid out. In June 1920, Air Vice-Marshal Sir W.G. Salmond, now of the Royal Air Force, formed on the 1st April 1918, visited Bahrain. He noted that the strip was too narrow and asked for it to be widened.

The first aircraft to land at Bahrain arrived from RAF Shaibah in Iraq on 8th June 1924 but it was not certain exactly which type of aircraft they were. The official records of the whole Iraq Command are missing from the Public Records Office in Kew including those of both No 84 and No 55 Squadrons who were based at Shaibah at that time. It is most likely that the three aircraft were De Havilland DH9As known as "Ninaks" belonging to Number 55 Squadron.

During this four-day public relations visit the Deputy Ruler, Sheikh Hamad bin Isa Al Khalifa, and the Political Agent were taken on a flight, which lasted one-and-a-half hours. For the first time, the Deputy Ruler viewed the 'whole of his dominions' from the air, and over-flew the Bahrain pearling fleet, which was then at work some forty miles from the main island.

During this period, No 203 Sqn, also based at Basra, carried out extensive reconnaissance flights around the whole coast of Arabia and down to the Horn of Africa. Today, the F16 Fighting Falcon provides a most credible deterrent force.

IN 1927, THE BRITISH FOREIGN OFFICE CONSIDERED THAT THERE WAS A REAL possibility that Russians might send troops to occupy the southern shore of Persia. As a result the Air Ministry and Imperial Airways jointly surveyed the Arabian side of the Persian Gulf including the territory of the Trucial Sheikhdoms. This was a wise decision because the Persians laid down a new corridor for aircraft across mountains over 10,000 feet high, salt deserts which turned into quagmires in winter and areas without roads, telegraph or wireless stations.

In the expectation of further obstacles being imposed by Persians, Imperial Airways went ahead with their plans to move their route to the Arabian side of the Gulf. During 1932, this new route, using the Handley Page HP 42, was opened to traffic. Much of the credit was due to Sheikh Issa who was on good terms with the RAF. He had the foresight to realise the potential of such traffic and persuaded most of the other Sheikhs to allow flying boats to alight along their coastlines and to co-operate in the construction of airfields for land planes. The island of Bahrain became a staging post for both types of aircraft. In the early 1930's, it became a common sight to see passengers waiting for aircraft sheltered in the barasti hut seen here. Public announcements were limited to the ringing of bells; four bells, aircraft about to approach; two bells, signal for passengers to embark; six bells: aircraft departing. This was a far cry from the ultra modern airport today.

BAHREIN MARINE AIRPORT

REVENUE FROM THE EMPIRE AIRMAIL SCHEME (EAMS) was essential to Imperial Airways who proposed to operate these routes with flying boats. The agreement of the British government to adopt the EAMS was ensured by the promise that the use of flying-boats would avoid the huge expense of enlarging existing aerodromes, many of which were often unserviceable during the monsoon seasons. The Air Ministry agreed to provide the marine facilities.

Short Brothers were asked to tender a design to meet the requirements and offered the 'C' class flying boat, an all-metal, high-wing monoplane. It had two decks, the upper one for the crew, the lower for 24 passengers, two stewards, luggage and mail. The passenger area was divided into three cabins. The forward one was a promenade cabin where passengers could stand and look out of the windows. Cruising speed was 165 mph and the original range specification was for 800 miles. Imperial Airways ordered 28 machines straight off the drawing board. Qantas Empire Airways and the New Zealand airline Tasman ordered a smaller number. The first of the new flying boats to go down its slipway and be taken up by Short's test pilot was Canopus on 4th July 1936. A 'Marine Airport' was already established at Gudaibiya, near the 'guest palace,' and used by the RAF. The first Empire arrived in Bahrain on 3rd October 1937 carrying passengers who had paid £274 (BD 164/-) for a return ticket from London to Sydney. The entire flight was supposed to take nine days, but the Company had difficulties keeping to the published timetable over a route that was 13,000 miles long. Today the "Marine Airport" is 1.2 km inland from the Grand Mosque near the Oman Khayham Hotel. It is still occupied and fitted with the original ceiling fans.

Out Of A Clear Blue Sky, Freddie Bosworth, A Retired Royal Air Force pilot arrived in Bahrain in his Avro Anson at the end of 1948. The Gulf Aviation Company, the forerunner of Gulf Air as we know it today, was first incorporated as a limited company on the 24th March 1949 in the State of Bahrain. The very first flight was to Muscat carrying just three passengers. The fare was 220 Gulf Rupees. Prior to this service, the only was to reach Muscat was by the British India Steam ship where the first class fare was 225 Gulf Rupees. Soon after, the first American built Constellations arrived, able to carry large numbers of passengers. The delivery of the latest Airbus A330 at the Paris Air Show was completed by the appearance of the renovated Anson.

THE FIRST BAHRAINI TO GAIN A COMMERCIAL pilots licence, in 1972, was Captain AbdulRahman Moh'd Algaud, now the Assistant Under-secretary for Aviation Services in Bahrain. Some little time before, in 1954, Flt Lt Jackie Moggridge was photographed whilst on a refuelling stop in Bahrain. Jackie was born in South Africa, where she was both the youngest woman to make a parachute jump and the Union's youngest woman pilot at the age of 17. In 1940, she went to Great Britain to join the Air Transport Auxiliary and delivered more aircraft than any other ATA pilot during the war. 300 of these deliveries were Spitfires. In 1954, she was recruited to ferry Spitfires out to the Burmese Air Force when this photograph was taken. Today, the fun in having a new uniform is apparent against a backdrop of the Avro Anson and the new Gulf Air A330 in Paris.

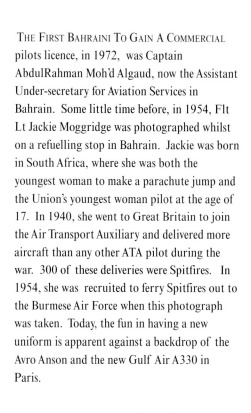

BAHRAIN INTERNATIONAL AIRPORT HAS COME A long way since the 1930s when an arrival bell hung outside a barusti hut. In those days, if twenty passengers arrived, this was a big crowd. Even in the 1950s, departing passengers took their belongings to the aircraft in a truck. Today more than three million passengers pass through Bahrain every year.

When the commemorative flight of the Vickers Vimy flew into the central area of Bahrain, it was escorted by the then Crown Prince in his personal helicopter. The celebration combined the replica of a traditional aircraft, pith helmets, welcoming royalty, splendid horsemen and an enthusiastic crowd.

Chapter 4
The Discovery of Oil

THE ARCHIVES TELL US IN THE GAZETTEER OF THE GULF that in 1908 a Mr J. G. Lorimer had found "A small deposit of asphalt penetrating the Pliocene rocks 3 miles south-south east of Jabal Al-Dukhan". A few years later, the British Admiral Sir Edmund Slade, made a two day expedition to the same A'ain Al-Ghar. The a'ain (a fresh water spring) owes its name to a smell of ghar (bitumen). Despite the reports, most "experts" were loud in their assertions that there were no worthwhile reserves of oil in Bahrain. Major Frank Holmes, a flamboyant New Zealander, who had come to Bahrain to drill artesian wells for the government, was convinced that oil was present and in 1930 the Bahrain Petroleum Company (BAPCO), was formed. In 1931, the company began test drilling south of Jebel Dukhan (Mountain of Smoke). On Christmas Day, 1932, news arrived in Manama of "great ponds of black oil and black rivulets flowing down the wadis. Oil, and what looked to us like smoke, but which was in fact gas, spouted gustily from the oil drilling rig and all the machinery, and the men who were working, were dripping with oil". The discovery could not have come at a more opportune time. Today the A'ain Al-Ghar is covered by a road and nearby is the oil museum. Close by is the first oil well, still pumping.

THE FIRST OIL EXPORTED WAS 40,000 TONS OF crude in 1934; this quadrupled to 170,000 in 1935, and almost quadrupled again in the following year. By the late 1930's output was 1 million tons annually. However, it was quickly realised that greater profit lay in shipping refined petroleum products. These were worth much more and occupied the same shipping volume. The first small refinery, with a capacity for about 10,000 barrels of crude oil per day, was completed in 1937, but the demand was so great that a second plant was immediately built alongside it. The two combined plants could refine some 25,000 barrels each day but by the outbreak of the Second World War, the Sitra refining complex was producing 33,000 barrels per day.

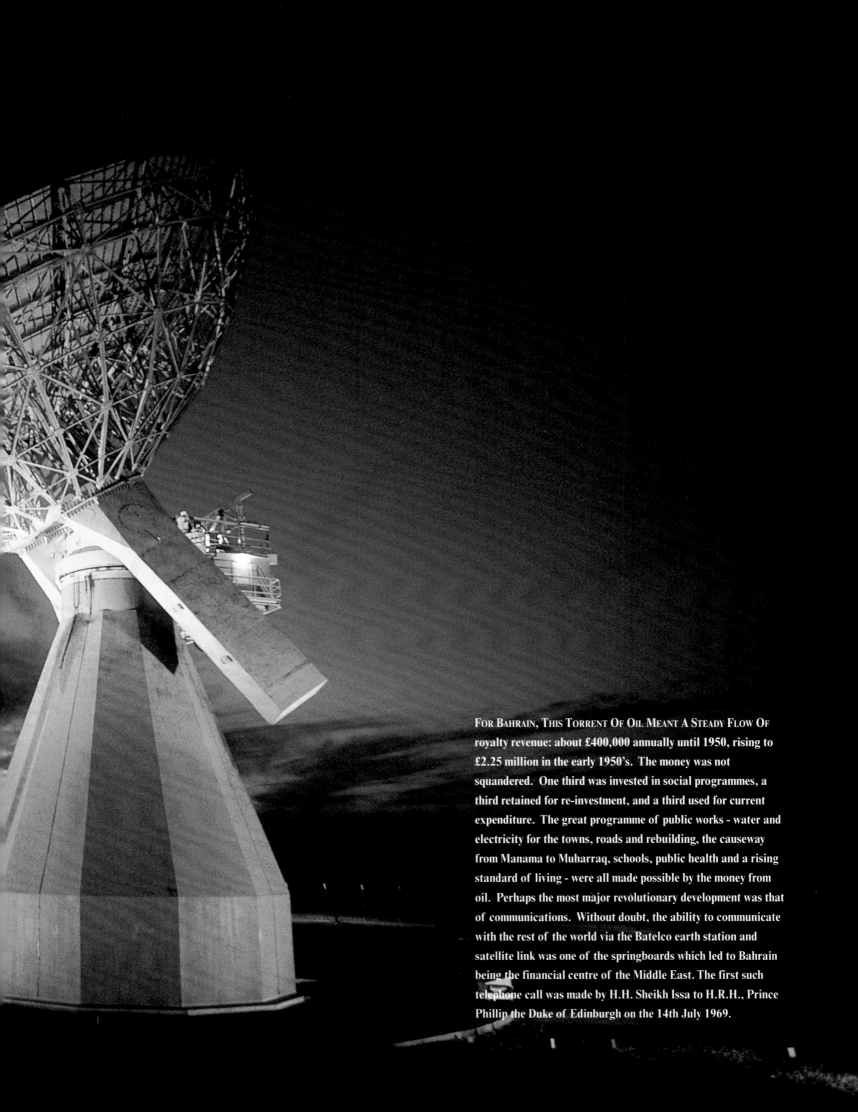

FOR BAHRAIN, THIS TORRENT OF OIL MEANT A STEADY FLOW OF royalty revenue: about £400,000 annually until 1950, rising to £2.25 million in the early 1950's. The money was not squandered. One third was invested in social programmes, a third retained for re-investment, and a third used for current expenditure. The great programme of public works - water and electricity for the towns, roads and rebuilding, the causeway from Manama to Muharraq, schools, public health and a rising standard of living - were all made possible by the money from oil. Perhaps the most major revolutionary development was that of communications. Without doubt, the ability to communicate with the rest of the world via the Batelco earth station and satellite link was one of the springboards which led to Bahrain being the financial centre of the Middle East. The first such telephone call was made by H.H. Sheikh Issa to H.R.H., Prince Phillip the Duke of Edinburgh on the 14th July 1969.

THE OUTPUT FROM THE FIRST REFINERY WAS simply insufficient to meet demand. To augment the oil production, more supplies were brought from Saudi Arabia. Barges full of crude were being brought from the Dhahran fields, until a pipeline was laid between the field and sitra in 1945. The Allies eagerly bought the output, more investment was poured into the Sitra site and by 1944, the vital high-grade aviation spirit was being produced for the war effort. well after the war a new pipeline was added and the oil wealth provided the means to build the causeway connecting the two countries, a vivid contrast from the dhows used previously.

THE DEMANDS BY THE OIL INDUSTRY FOR urgent parts and equipment led to the development of the air express carriers. In 1974, DHL became the first carrier to establish a regional distribution centre in Bahrain to serve the surrounding region. In the early days, DHL operated from a tiny dome shaped hangar. Such was the demand and equally, such was the swift response, that now the DHL B 757 dedicated freighter operates between Brussels and Bahrain on a daily basis. A fleet of smaller aircraft then distributes the express cargo around the region, a far cry from freight being offloaded from dhows.

THE DISCOVERY OF OIL BROUGHT OIL WORKERS FROM around the Gulf and around the World. The game of golf was just one of the many new games that arrived with them. Initially, golf was played from "browns" but in an area between the pipelines and nodding donkeys, a new green course has been developed. The Riffa Golf Club has transformed more than 150 acres of desert into a green oasis of sporting excellence. The 6,875-yard, par 72 golf course has over 600 palm trees and 400 specimen trees as well as five salt-water lakes and 70 sand bunkers.

Chapter 5
The Capital - Manama

THESE AERIAL VIEWS OF BAHRAIN CLEARLY SHOW how the shape of Bahrain has changed over the last fifty years. Land reclamation has increased the available land area by several square kilometres permitting the building of an entire new district, the so-called Diplomatic area. Land reclamation is set to continue simply because this prosperous nation is simply running out of existing available land.

FROM THE TOP OF THE NATIONAL BANK OF BAHRAIN, below and left lies the Bab Al Bahrain, the main gate to the once walled town where the streets of the souq teem with gold, carpets, rainbows of cloth, brassware, the ubiquitous jeans and now a vast selection of international airline tickets. From this angle, it is difficult to imagine that half of this picture, from the Bab Al Bahrain towards the right, was originally the sea. The dhow harbour has progressively shifted to its present location. Beyond the Inter Continental Hotel, in the distance, is the pearl roundabout and the new road leading to the Le Royal Meridien Hotel.

THE DEVELOPMENT OF MANAMA. THIS SEQUENCE of photographs shows the stages of development in the centre of Manama. The archives reveal that in the early 1920's, the first sight of Manama from the sea was of "a squat line of mud-coloured houses along the shore with no buildings of any height, no minarets and nothing green." In other parts of the town, there were grander buildings, but the seafront was unimpressive, and it was here that the rebuilding of Manama was begun. By the early 1930's, a new Customs House was erected, and new jetties were built. A fountain was laid down and a courthouse constructed; this now houses the Directorate of Heritage. In 1945, the square was completed with the construction of a ceremonial gateway, the formal entrance to the state - Bab al Bahrain. The building was used as government offices, and Sheikh Salman bin Hamad had his office there. Behind Bab al Bahrain the souq and the commercial district grew.

BESIDES THE BAB AL BAHRAIN, THE YATEEM
Mosque is perhaps the most beautiful symbol of
Bahrain. This area marks the boundary between
the old and the new. The site was originally
occupied by the first petrol station in Bahrain.
Of all the sights, this was the symbol of the
turning point that was reached following the
discovery of oil. Before a more extensive road
network was built, donkey carts provided a
distribution system for the outlying villages.

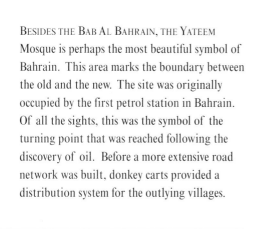

THEN, IN THE EARLY 1920'S, IT WAS NOTED THAT "THERE WAS AN IDEA OF building a causeway linking Manama to Muharraq." In the 1930s, work began on the building of the causeway, initially, simply as two walls of flat seastone infilled with rubble. The steel sections of the swing bridge, which spanned the deep-water channel, were manufactured three times in England during the early part of the Second World War but the first two delivery ships were sunk. The final delivery was made in 1942 and the swing bridge operated perfectly to allow large dhows to pass down the channel.

Although the causeway was very narrow, allowing only one way traffic controlled by policeman, its opening revolutionised contact between the two main islands. The dhow captains were vigorously opposed to it since their livelihood was at stake but the majority welcomed this new marvel of communication. Today, the tollhouse still exists now occupied by the Coastguard. The old price to cross was four annas for a taxi, six annas for a bus with pedestrians and private cars crossing free. Now there are two causeways with a third about to be built linking the Hidd area to the Grand mosque crossroads.

THIS IS A VIEW THAT IS IMPOSSIBLE TO FIND ON old photographs because it simply never existed before land reclamation. Almost all the land and buildings encompassed by this photographed are built on land reclaimed since 1960. Before that time, when the sun had set, there was nothing but black sea. Today the area glows with ribbons of light from commuting cars.

Chapter 6
The Advance of Industry

THE NEW SEAPORT AT MINA SALMAN, WHICH WAS OPENED IN 1958, WAS BUILT for international traffic. The shoals and reefs around Manama harbour had always made it awkward as a centre for steamship trade. Only trading dhows could get alongside where their cargoes of goats sometimes became self-unloading. Increasingly, cargo ships had discharged their cargoes on Sitra Island, and these were carried round to Manama by sea. Mina Salman provided a deep-water anchorage accessible to both Manama and Muharraq.

THE BRITISH INDIA STEAM NAVIGATION COMPANY was formed in 1862 by Sir William MacKinnon to extend his India service to include Basra and Bahrain. The principal purpose was for the transport of ordinary sea mail, considered vital by the British Government to maintain communications throughout the British Empire. Bahrain provided the safest haven of the Gulf for traditional sailing vessels, but the shallow water and many shoals and reefs made it hazardous for steamships. A short stone pier was constructed in 1901; prior to this, visitors waded onto the beach, or climbed onto one of the white donkeys for which Bahrain was famous, and then splashed through the shallows to the shore. Later the pier was extended to a length of a quarter of a mile, and a parallel jetty constructed for landing cargo. However, plans to dredge a deep-water anchorage were never accomplished in Manama, and attention switched to Sitra Island where the oil refinery was located in the mid-1930's. In the 1950s, three steamers were operating, the Dwarka, the Dahressa and the Dahra which sank off Sharjah in 1963. The number of passengers who embarked in Bahrain was very small compared with the thousands of passengers who arrive and depart every day on the sleek modern jet airliners of Gulf Air today.

Sparks still fly in the back of the souq but the Bahrain government realised that it had to make more diverse use of its oil income. ALBA (Aluminium Bahrain) was one of these projects and the foundation stone was laid in 1969. It is today one of the world's largest, most modern, aluminium smelters with an annual capacity of over 500,000 tonnes. In producing aluminium, ALBA formed the origin of a series of aluminium users such as the Gulf Aluminium Rolling Mill Company (GARMCO), the Bahrain Aluminium Extrusion Company (BALEXCO) and Bahrain Atomisers International (BAI) who produce 6,000 tonnes of aluminium powder each year.

THERE ARE MANY TYPES OF DATES IN BAHRAIN, some yellow and others red skinned. They were noted for their succulence and in a study of dental diseases, it appears that Early Dilmun people ate dates, other fruits, vegetables, meat and fish with grain products constituting a minor part of the diet. Bahrain was long known as the "land of a million palm trees". The products of the palm, from the dates themselves, through the fronds and branches used to make barasti shelters, and the palm trunks, used to make beams and lintels in large buildings, were crucial to Bahrain's economy. Since the mid 1800s, HP (Houses of Parliament) sauce, that essential part of an Englishman's diet, has contained dates in the closely guarded recipe.

TRADITIONAL FISHING METHODS CONTINUE TODAY. THERE are three general types in use. The first is the hand thrown traditional net still observed around the shores of Bahrain. The second type is the *Hadra* fish trap, a deceptively simple device constructed out from the shore. Fish are guided into a heart-shaped maze where they are left as the tide recedes. There are many such traps all around the coast of Bahrain. The third type is the *Gargour* trap. These igloo shaped traps were originally made of palm leaves but are now made of wire with cement block wieghts. The traps are baited with rotting fish, which entices fish to enter through a one-way funnel-like opening. Larger fish cannot escape due to the tapering narrow entrance though smaller fish can escape to provide the fish stocks for another day. These traps are deployed from the fishing dhows that set sail every afternoon. The fishermen are primarily out to catch *hamour* (grouper) and *gobab* (tuna). Other fish that are caught include *hamra* (red snapper), *shari* (emperor) and *jersh* (jacks). The prize catch is *zubedi* (silver pomfret) which is one of the most expensive fishes in the *souq*. Inland, fertile areas of northern Bahrain sustained good crops of wheat.

THE BRITISH BANK OF IRAN AND THE MIDDLE EAST

THE STRATEGIC GEOGRAPHICAL POSITION OF Bahrain caused the country to become the main redistribution centre of the Gulf States and the entire Middle East. The British Bank of Iran and The Middle East was opened by the Emir in 1944 and led the way to Bahrain becoming the financial centre of the Middle East. The need for educated Nationals led to the establishment of Bahrain University on an extensive campus. Their long- term contributions will ensure Bahrain's strategic position in the world of trade and finance.

JIDDA ISLAND IS A UNIQUE LOCATION WHERE THE sandstone blocks for the Barbar Temple (see p.18) were quarried. the island was used continuously over the centuries and also the stone for the Portuguese Fort was quarried here, then carried by dhow to the mainland. Until 1990, the island was used as a prison, the buildings being clearly visible on the ariel photograph. The picture also shows how the sea was eroding the sand stone overhangs. Today Jidda Island has been protected and landscaped. It is now a haven for migrating and resident birds. During a brief visit, ornithologist Howard King,

recorded more than fifty different species including *Alcedo atthis* (Common Kingfisher), *Tringa hypoleucos* (Common Sandpiper), *Accipiter nisus* (Eurasian Sparrowhawk), *Phalacrocorax carbo* (Great Cormorant) and *Pycnonotus leucogenys* (White cheeked Bulbul). The dhows that carried the huge stones gave rise to another industry of shipbuilding and repair. Recently the Arab Shipbuilding repair Yard (ASRY) docked and repaired an ULCC which was 182 metres long, the longest vessel ever repaired during the 21 years of ASRY operations.

Chapter 7
Sports & Tourism

THEN, ONE DONNED A PITH HELMET FOR A FISHING trip out in the bays around Bahrain. Now, tourists wear a secure harness before being lifted over 100 metres into the air. Suspended beneath the parachute, the flyer has a splendid bird's eye view of a traditional fishing dhow.

FOR MANY CENTURIES, THE TRAINING OF WILD FALCONS to prey on bustards or hare, has been a sporting tradition in the Gulf. The original need was a basic one for food though now falconry is practised in Bahrain as a sport. The birds, saker or peregrine falcons, are snared on their southbound migration in the autumn. The birds are then trained and used for hunting before being released to return to their northern breeding grounds. Horses and camels have always had a special fascination for the people of Bahrain and indeed for all Arab people. The horse for pride of ownership and the camel, not only as a beast of burden but also for another remarkable ability. The camel is able to drink brackish water that no human could drink and turn it into the finest nourishing milk. It was by the use of the camel that the Bedouin were able to traverse great distances to trade.

FOOTBALL IS PLAYED THROUGHOUT BAHRAIN. In 1960, it was played in front of the Palace before the area was covered with tarmac. Today, football is played against the backdrop of Riffa Fort, which was built in 1812 by Sheikh Salman bin Ahmad al Fateh. It was used as the seat of government and as his residence. There are square towers on each corner and a circular tower to the Northwest. The fort was recently renovated when it was discovered that the fort was built on the site of a former fort built around 1700.

BAHRAIN HAS ONE OF THE BEST RACECOURSES IN the Middle East. Located adjacent to Medinat Hamad, the course has a grass track — the first in the Gulf, an artificial lake and a grandstand for 10,000 spectators. It was opened in 1981 to replace a smaller track overlooked by Riffa Fort. Sheikh Sulman introduced thoroughbred horse racing in the 1940s, a tradition maintained by the Amiri stud who ride in bright red colours.

THE TRADITIONAL SOUQ WAS LOCATED BEHIND THE Bab Al Bahrain where the traditional street layout is still visible. Here, all general trade, money changing and shopping was conducted until modern shopping malls could be built on the reclaimed land. The basic need for food and many other luxury items is now fulfilled by modern shopping malls complete with 24 hour Automated Teller Machines.

BEING AN ISLAND, SWIMMING HAS ALWAYS BEEN A necessary skill for the inhabitants of Bahrain. In days gone by, Bahrainis swam at the Adari Pools. Today, swimmers enjoy luxurious pools while in the background, para fliers swoop over the lagoon.

ABU MAHIR FORT WAS BUILT ON A SMALL ROCKY
island which took its name from an
underground natural spring. Sheikh Abdullah
bin Ahmed Al Khalifa built the fort in 1840 but
British warships largely destroyed it in 1868. It
was restored in 1980 and now is part of the HQ
of the Bahrain Coastguard. The bay in front of
the fort is the arena for the annual Bahrain
Open Championship Aquabike Grand Prix of
the Middle East and Asia. The annual event is
held under the patronage of the Crown Prince
and President of the Supreme Council for Youth
and Sports Sheikh Salman bin Hamad Al
Khalifa. The world's best Jet Ski champions
mounted on 1200cc Jet Skis provide spectacular
racing.

Chapter 8
Natural History
& Culture

THEN & NOW — THE NATIONAL DAY OF Bahrain. Traditional dancing, though still widely practised, has been supplemented by spectacular displays of fireworks.

THE TREE OF LIFE, BOTANICALLY CLASSIFIED AS A
Prosopis juliflora, and captured on canvas by
David Shepherd. Today, the gazelles have gone
but the tree continues to flourish. The
irrigation source of this isolated member of
the bean family, a relative of the Central
American mesquite tree, still remains a
mystery.

BAIT SHEIKH ISA IS A FINE BEAUTIFULLY RESTORED example of a traditional Bahraini courtyard house. Built by the great great grandfather of the present Amir, this was the family home in the centre of Muharraq, which was the capital at the time. Also restored is the old fort at Riffa in contrast with the many old houses which have disappeared completely during modernisation.

AL JASRA IS ONLY A SMALL VILLAGE ON THE WEST Coast of Bahrain but a significant one for the people of Bahrain. Bait Al Jasra was the birthplace of the late Amir. The house was built in 1907 using the available materials - coral stone, gypsum, and mangrove poles with matting made from date palm fronds. The house was restored in 1986 as a heritage museum and nearby the Al-Jasra Handicraft Centre was established in 1990. The main objective of the Al-Jasra Handicraft Centre is to preserve the national identity of Bahrain's heritage.

FROM A TIME BEFORE MAN ARRIVED, THE SOCOTRA CORMORANT (Phalacrocorax nigrogularis) (top right) has migrated and bred in vast numbers on the Hawar Islands. These vast colonies, — more than 250,000 birds— breed during late autumn and winter and are now fortunate to be a protected species in a National Park. Around the islands the three meter-long dugong, (Dugong dugong), grazes on the seagrass beds, an environment shared with the Pacific humpback dolphin (Sousa sinensis). Fishing is banned within the National Park and hence fish stocks are plentiful for winged occupants such as the Osprey (Pandion haliaetus) and the Sooty Falcon (Falco concolor) (top left). Then, in former times, the inhabitants of Bahrain collected both the cormorant eggs and its nestlings. Now, the Hawar Islands are protected though tourists can visit the resorts and enjoy this wonderful eco system.

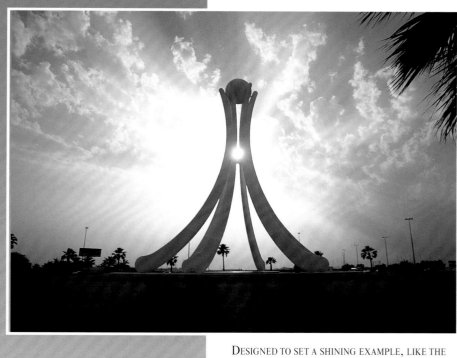

DESIGNED TO SET A SHINING EXAMPLE, LIKE THE Pearl Monument, the Bait Al Quran was built by the Bahrain government to be a public centre of excellence in the study of the Koran. This unique building now protects a vast collection of priceless, original Korans collected from world-wide sources. These exquisite documents are not only valuable originals but also works of art in their own right. Many of these treasures were produced by hand before the advent of the printing press and show the art of calligraphy.

Chapter 9
Authors
Acknowledgements

Having published "Now & Then - The Emirates", I knew that there was a wealth of old photographs of Bahrain. An invitation to set up a seaplane operation led to numerous visits to Bahrain allowing time to explore this wonderful island. It also led to meeting the people of Bahrain, both expatriates and Nationals. I'm pleased to say that without exception, there was tremendous enthusiasm for the project. With such encouragement, the project progressed relatively smoothly with only one major upset when I was unable to be in two places at the same time! David Woodward, the General Manager of Le Royal Meridien Hotel once remarked that I was always happy with a smile on my face. On reflection, he was quite correct and this situation was the direct result of meeting so many charming and helpful people of all nationalities. Add a sprinkling of absolute characters and I can report that there was never a dull moment. I received a great deal of help from many officials, in particular; His Highness Sheikh Khalifa bin Salman Al Khalifa, The Prime Minister, who kindly arranged for the loan of the old aerial photograph of Jidda Island and my visit to the island sanctuary; His Excellency Sheikh Ali Bin Khalifa Al Khalifa, the Minister of Transportation, His Excellency Sheikh Khalid Bin Abdulla Al Khalifa, who kindly wrote the foreword and Sheikh Hussan bin Essa Al Khalifa of the Ministry of

Housing & Environment and the personnel on their staff, Peter Muijrers, Willem De Roo, Ahmed Reffat, Abbas A. Al Watani and especially Howard King whose detailed report "The Breeding Birds of The Hawar Islands" deserves special mention. Thanks go to Ahmed Al Sherooqi, Assistant Undersecretary for Press and Publications at The Ministry of Information for his valuable comments. Readers may also be interested to read the following books: "The Visitor's Guide to Bahrain Birds" by Michael & Mike Hill; "The House of Kanoo" by Mr Khalid Kanoo; "The Scorpions Sting – A History of 84 Squadron" by Don Neate; "Portrait in Oil" by Berry Ritchie in addition to "The GCC States, National Development Records" by Archive Editions, edited by A.L.P. Burdett. Professor Dan Potts of the School of Archeology, University of Sydney; Roy G. Leask, Naser Mohamed Naser and Salah Addeen Saeed of the National Bank of Bahrain and Salman S. Al-Mahmeed. One person deserves a special mention and he is His Excellency Yousef Ahmed Al Shirawi who not only gave his time but also provided access to his archives, including the Belgrave archives plus the support of his staff and an office in which I could work. All the modern maps are available at the Ministry of Housing or at the GIS Dept in the Centre for Remote Sensing, at a modest cost.